T0113864

# AROUND YOUR
# HOUSE
## WITHOUT YOUR
# SPOUSE

### Learning to Live
### on Your Own Again

DAVID PATTON

WESTBOW
PRESS®
A DIVISION OF THOMAS NELSON
& ZONDERVAN

WestBow Press books may be ordered through booksellers or by contacting:

WestBow Press
A Division of Thomas Nelson & Zondervan
1663 Liberty Drive
Bloomington, IN 47403
www.westbowpress.com
844-714-3454

Scripture quotations taken from The Holy Bible, New International Version® NIV® Copyright © 1973 1978 1984 2011 by Biblica, Inc. TM. Used by permission. All rights reserved worldwide.

ISBN: 978-1-6642-9035-8 (sc)
ISBN: 978-1-6642-9249-9 (e)

Library of Congress Control Number: 2023902882

Print information available on the last page.

WestBow Press rev. date: 02/13/2023

Dedicated to Kim and Scott in
memory of their mother, Janet.

This is my family from our 50th Wedding Anniversary

# Contents

# Foreword

## By Scott Patton

Experiencing illness, injury, and death with a loved one is never easy, and often the last thing people want to hear in the moment is that "it happens for a reason." In the moment, we want the pain to go away, we want the injury to be healed, and we want more time with our loved ones. In time, you will see that all things *do* happen for a reason, but you may not know it in the moment—or for quite a while after.

My mother fell and broke her ankle and then was not able to carry on with the normal routines that she and my father had established over fifty-three years of marriage. As with all relationships that have developed over time, everyone has a role to play. Someone is responsible for making the coffee, someone is responsible for paying the bills, someone is responsible for sending birthday cards, and the list goes on and on. When my mother fell, my father suddenly had to fill both roles.

God blessed my parents with two years of training before my mother went to be with the Lord. What a gift to have the time to learn new tasks and prepare for a new chapter. While it is hard to see at the moment, I can promise that a broken ankle was a true blessing that happened for a reason. Watching my father take in his new routines is a testament to the love my mother showed in the final years preparing him for the future.

A simple system of three-by-five cards was the perfect way for my mother to "train" my father. The old saying "You can't teach an old dog new tricks" is simply not true. You just need some time, patience, and three-by-five cards.

# Introduction

We had a traditional marriage for fifty-five years with traditional roles. I handled the financial role, and Janet handled the household role. Everything worked because everyone had their role.

Upon my retirement, we moved to a new area, new lifestyle, and the same roles. We enjoyed traveling to visit children, grandchildren, family members, and friends.

Our roles didn't change when I had prostate cancer and Janet developed cancer. We didn't see the warning signs. That changed when Janet broke her ankle in three places and her cancer came back.

Even with all the early chances and even more time due to being retired, the broken ankle and the cancer were the catalyst that made me aware the roles would change and turn my life upside down. That's when I started using my three-by-five white cards to learn about Janet's roles. Lesson learned. Take time to do this *before* your spouse passes. My hope and prayer for writing this is to help you prepare for this and make your life a little bit less stressful.

I know that every relationship has different roles, every house has different appliances, financial situations can be extremely complex or relatively simple, and everyone has their own personal beliefs. Now is the time, while you still have *your* expert with you, to teach each other as much as you can. Is it a little bit scary? Yes. Can it be intimidating? Yes. Is it absolutely necessary? Yes. Can you, do it? Yes! You have an expert next to you to teach you everything he or she knows.

## Chapter 1

# HOUSEHOLD

For fifty-five years, I never had to cook, do laundry, use a dishwasher, etc. Like I said, we both had our roles and it worked for us. In the following areas, I will detail what I learned about Janet's roles that I previously had taken for granted. Now I don't proclaim to be an expert and still have a lot to learn, but it has been fun learning a whole new set of skills. The following are a few areas and tips to consider as you get started:

1. Laundry (Washer and Dryer)
    a. Settings, temperatures, heat, etc.
    b. Sorting towels and sheets from clothes, and which require hot, not warm settings.
    c. Detergent levels.
    d. Which clothes do not go in the dryer?
    e. Length of time to dry clothes.

It was very intimidating looking at all those knobs, not realizing how and when to use them. A place for laundry soap and a different place for fabric softener—what a concept! When there was lint on some of my shirts, I had trouble using a lint remover, even with the help of my children, Kim and Scott. I had many amusing attempts learning how to use it. I still haven't mastered it yet, but I am committed to becoming a professional.

Here is an example of two of my three-by-five cards:

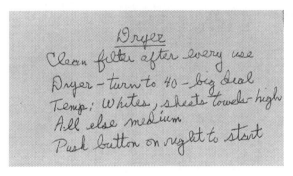

This is an example of my dryer card

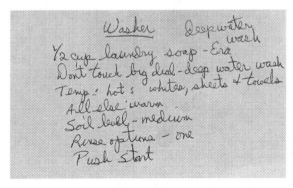

This is an example of my washer card

Pro tip: Fitted sheets. Mark the top two corners with a little black marker so you can always find them. I know now why Janet wanted my help to fold the sheets. She was teaching me even without knowing it. You could probably create a funny YouTube video on my experiences doing this.

2.  Dishwasher
    a.  How to load items.
    b.  Detergents to use and where to put them.
    c.  What not to put in the dishwasher (very important).
    d.  Settings on the dial.

I quickly learned why we never left the house with it running. I came back from my daily walk, only to find water all over the kitchen floor. The drainpipe had come loose. Thank goodness we lived in an apartment during retirement. Maintenance was able to come and fix it. Lesson learned!

3.  Microwave
    a.  Learn all the settings, including shortcuts (e.g., thirty seconds instead of cook time and numbers start).
    b.  Items that shouldn't go in a microwave (e.g., foil, plastic-to-go containers, and metal).
    c.  Paper plates.

Probably the most useful appliance and by far the most used.

4. Oven/Stove
   a. Settings, temperature controls, and timer.
   b. What not to put in the oven (e.g., paper products).

Pro tip: If the smoke alarm should go off for any mysterious reason, grab a towel and wave it vigorously until it stops.

5. Telephone
   a. How to retrieve voicemail messages.
   b. How to use call waiting.
   c. How to transfer landline to cell phone when leaving the house.
   d. How to change favorite numbers.
   e. Phone number of the telephone company provider.

6. TV/DVR
   a. Learn to use the remote.
   b. Learn how to record programs then play them.
   c. If you have a streaming service, such as Hulu or Firestick by Amazon, learn what to use and when to use the remote that came with the TV.
   d. Phone number of cable provider.

7. Pantry/Cupboards/Refrigerator/Freezer
   a. Expiration dates: We had some items up to three years old. Even if unopened, don't ignore these expiration dates.
   b. Clean out and give away items that you are unlikely to ever use.

My daughter's favorite question was "Dad, are you ever going to use this?" If not, then throw it out.

Friends who are likely to use unexpired items are very appreciative of receiving them.

8. Cooking
   a. Learn what pans to use for what you are making.
   b. Start with simplest items (e.g., grilled cheese and scrambled eggs).

If you haven't had to do these simple things for fifty-five years, it is quite overwhelming. My support system in this area includes Kim, Scott, and my brother. All were very patient with me. I know they must have been thinking, *Wow. He really doesn't know how to do what we take for granted.*

9. Other miscellaneous items to consider. We lived in an apartment so some of these didn't apply. Like I said, every house is different, and your cards should look different from mine.

a. How to turn the water on/off to the house.

b. How to start and operate the lawn mower and other lawn equipment.

c. How to turn off the water heater.

d. How to use technology in the house. (Some may be automated.)

e. How to reset the WI-FI router.

f. How to use the tools that are in garage or shed.

g. When to drip the water during a freeze.

h. How to clean the air and water filters.

i. Passwords to spouse's phone, computers, bank accounts, insurance policies, and investments.

j. How to access any social media accounts for your spouse.

Pro tip: Write the usernames and passwords for any accounts, and keep them on the three-by-five card. Be sure to keep this card hidden or secure from anyone who is working or visiting your home.

## Chapter 2

# FINANCIAL

This area was unfamiliar to Janet due to me being an accountant by trade. This can be very overwhelming for someone who is not familiar with this role. One time the bank called and informed Janet that the mortgage was late. She said, "It is never late because my husband is an accountant." She never let me live that down as it was actually late.

1.  Paying Bills

    Make sure your spouse knows where you keep your bills and records. If they are in a filing cabinet or in a divided box of any kind, or if there is some type of system that has been created, make sure they can access them and know the system. They should learn to pay current bills as they come each month. It is also important to learn to retrieve older credit card statements if any issues or questions on

payments arise. Keeping receipts from stores and matching with statements ensures you were charged the right amount.

2.  Credit and Debit Cards

    Make a list of credit cards that you have: joint, yours, and hers (or his). Don't forget usernames and passwords if the accounts are set up online and any PIN numbers that are associated with the cards. If an issue arises, be sure your spouse knows where to find them and how to access them. Learn together why credit scores are important and what can impact them.

3.  Banking

    Make a list of bank accounts, any certificates of deposit, and safe deposit box. Be sure your spouse knows where the keys are kept to the safe deposit box and that you both have access to it.

4.  Financial Advisor

    Show them where you keep statements from your financial advisor. Include them in conversations and meetings with your advisor. It's important that they are comfortable with your advisor, how to contact them, and trust that they have your best interests and objectives clearly understood.

5. Life Insurance

   A list of all your life insurance policies and where they are kept. I suggest a small house safe. List the agents' names and telephone numbers to the policies.

6. There are several other legal documents that need to be drawn up by lawyers.

   a. Wills.

   b. Durable power of attorney.

   c. Medical directives, including DNR or not.

These are important and critical documents that should be prepared. Keep in mind they need to be revised if you move from state to state. Having multiple copies can help when you need to access them in a hurry. Many medical providers will require their own copies for their files.

Pro tip: Have your spouse pay the bills for a month, have a meeting with your financial advisor, and always keep these records secure.

## Chapter 3

# FUNERAL ARRANGEMENTS AND IMPACT ON FAMILY

I am so glad that we had discussed and made funeral arrangements before time. I can't imagine having to decide all these things on the spur of the moment. It's stressful enough time without trying to make rational decisions. It guarantees you get what you want. No family members want to talk about it or pay for it. But it is inevitable and should be addressed, even though it's difficult, beforehand.

The following should be addressed at a minimum:

1. Cemetery plots.
2. Funeral home prepay.
3. Pastor.
4. Songs.
5. Scriptures.

6. Photos to be converted to a slideshow.
7. Contacts to be advised of passing.

Discussing with your children your desire beforehand is so important. It avoids trouble and potential issues that could arise between you or your children. You don't want your children to not speak to each other over these issues. Unfortunately, we have seen this in our family and other families that we know. We will rest easier knowing that we have made our desires clear and no problems will occur.

Pro tip: Share with immediate family where your plans are for your funeral so they will know whom to contact. These should be in a location that is accessible by family.

## Chapter 4

# MOVING FORWARD: MENTAL HEALTH

Mental health is something that you need to be aware of during this difficult time. I needed to have a support group of friends and family to share my feelings. I go and visit Janet every week after eating in our favorite restaurant.

Some things that should be remembered include the following:

1. Always remember the good times.
2. Symptoms that are normal in varying degrees.
   a. Feelings of sadness and tearfulness. (It's OK to cry; that is why God gave us tear ducts.)
   b. Feelings of emptiness and hopelessness. We must go on, even if it is difficult.
   c. Insomnia or sleeping too much.

d. Tiredness and lack of energy.

e. Anxiety and restlessness; be strong and active.

f. Slowed thinking, speaking, or walking. Your deceased spouse would want you to go on.

g. Make plans to eat with friends. It helps fill the void.

h. Make travel plans to visit children (and remember they are grieving too). Also consider visiting other relatives.

i. Stress is normal, but don't let it get you down and affect your physical well-being.

j. Don't play the what-if game. God is in control and his plan was carved out. This is important and can get to us mentally, and we can't change anything.

When talking to other widows and widowers at church, the consensus is that you never get over it, no matter how long your spouse has been gone. One widow said, "You don't know or can't imagine what it is like until it happens to you." How true this is. The oddest things can trigger those feelings of sadness and loneliness. But the old saying is true. "Life is for the living."

Pro tip: Be aware of your mental state, and reach out for help when needed. Stay connected with friends and family.

Chapter 5

# MOVING FORWARD: PHYSICAL HEALTH

Physical health aspects can be just as important as mental health. Prior to Janet's passing, we kept physically active by walking outside or on the treadmill. This was not her favorite activity, but it was necessary. Since being on my own, I have become much more intentional about my physical activity. "Use it or lose it" is real. It is easy to find reasons to not "use it" some days, but having some small goals can keep you motivated. Some things to consider in this area include the following:

1. Keep being active, which could mean walking, going to a grocery store, or finding a friend to walk with.
2. Don't sit too long at the house. Continue to move around the house. I have a friend who once walked 10,000 steps in his house!

3. Eat properly and stay healthy.

4. Fresh air is very helpful.

5. Be active. Give yourself a few goals or tasks for each day.

6. Fitbit: My children got me one and I resisted at first. Now it is a part of my everyday life. It measures your steps, heart rate, etc. It is a great tool for being active.

7. Life Alert: This is a medical alert system specifically designed to help us in a home health emergency. It is especially helpful if your children are out of state. I haven't done this yet; however, I do share with them my location through my phone.

Pro tip: Stay active for your own well-being and physical health. Have accountability with either a friend or family member.

## Chapter 6

# SPIRITUAL/FAITH

This area could by far be the most important aspect of being able to move forward alone. However, remember you are not alone as you have God on your side. We often talked about how great it was to have faith and we were unsure how those without it made it through these difficult times. Some things to remember are the following:

1.  Above all else, remember that God is in control and has a plan for us. We might not know it until we see him face-to-face.
2.  If God doesn't answer our prayers the way we want, remember that it isn't part of his plan for us. Sometimes his answers are yes, no, or wait.
3.  Remember your favorite Bible verses, and say them over and over. Mine is Philippians 4:13. "I can do all things through Christ who gives me strength."

Some other verses that I found to be helpful are the following:

1. John 3:16

   For God so loved the world, that He gave His only begotten Son, that whosoever believeth in Him should not perish, but have everlasting life.

2. Psalm 23

   The Lord is my Shepherd, I shall lack nothing. He makes me to lie down in green pastures, He leads me beside the quiet waters He refreshes my soul. He guides me along the right paths for his name's sake. Even though I walk through the darkest valley, I will fear no evil, for you are with me. You prepare a table before me in the presence of my enemies. You anoint my head with oil.; my cup overflows. Surely goodness and love will follow me all the days of my life, and I will dwell in the house of the Lord forever.

3. Philippians 4:6

   Do not be anxious about anything, but in every situation, by prayer and petition, with thanksgiving, present your request to God.

4. Deuteronomy 31:8

   The Lord himself goes before you and will be with you; He will never leave you nor forsake you. Do not be afraid; do not be discouraged.

5.   1 Corinthians 10:13

No temptation has overtaken you except what is common to humankind. And God is faithful; he will not let you be tempted beyond what you can bear. But when you are tempted, He will also provide a way out so that you can endure it.

Pro tip: Another way of looking at time is not to remember how long since we've lost our spouses. Instead, think how it is another day closer to when we will be reunited with our spouses in heaven (not so easy).

# Conclusion

I started this process from a conversation with a friend from church expressing sympathy for losing Janet and asking me how I was doing. I explained the three-by-five cards, and she said, "You should write a book."

I started it in July 2022, and in telling my children about it, they encouraged me to do it. In November when I visited my son and family for Thanksgiving, we added more chapters and had a mini typed book. We distributed this to several close friends, and they thought it was great and helpful.

Then I discussed it with my pastor, and he liked it. he said, "David, I think you have something good there." We next had a Senior Adult Ministry development meeting, and everyone encouraged me to publish it.

I hope you enjoy the book and my story. But my real hope and prayer is that you take the next steps, however small they may be, to prepare yourself for the loss of your spouse.

God bless you.

David Patton

Printed in the United States
by Baker & Taylor Publisher Services